J 371.1

Stienecker, David $15.93

A frontier teacher 30440

DATE DUE

DEC 0 6 1995			
DEC 2 6 1995			
JAN 0 4 1996			
JAN 2 6 1996			
MAR 1 4 1996			

Washington Public Library
116 E. 2nd
Washington, KS 66968

HOW THEY LIVED

A FRONTIER TEACHER

DAVID STIENECKER

Illustrated by
Virginia Kylberg

Washington Library
116 E. 2nd
Washington, KS 66968

ROURKE BOOK COMPANY, INC.
Vero Beach, Florida 32964

Text © 1994 Rourke Book Company, Inc.
PO Box 3328, Vero Beach, Florida 32964

All rights reserved. No part of this book may be reproduced or utilized in any form or by any means, electronic or mechanical including photocopying, recording, or by any information storage and retrieval system without permission in writing from the publisher.

A Blackbirch Graphics book.

Printed in the United States of America.

Library of Congress Cataloging-in-Publication Data

Stienecker, David, 1952–
    A frontier teacher / David Stienecker; illustrated by Virginia Kylberg.
      p. cm. — (How they lived)
    Includes index.
    ISBN 1-55916-039-X
    1. Teachers—United States—History—19th century—Juvenile literature. 2. Rural schools—United States—History—19th century—Juvenile literature. 3. Frontier and pioneer life—United States—History—Juvenile literature. [1. Teachers—History. 2. Schools—History. 3. Frontier and pioneer life.] I. Title. II. Series: How they lived (Vero Beach, Fla.)
LB1775.2.S75   1994
371.1'00973'09034—dc20   94-742
                                                                       CIP
                                                                        AC

Printed in the USA

CONTENTS

A FRONTIER SCHOOL DAY 4

TRAVELING TO THE FRONTIER 6

WHAT THE LAND WAS LIKE 8

MAKING A HOME 10

FINDING A TEACHER 12

HOW A TEACHER LIVED 14

THE ONE-ROOM SCHOOLHOUSE 16

SCHOOL SUPPLIES 18

THE STUDENTS 20

TEACHING THE CLASS 22

WHEN SCHOOL WAS OUT 24

HAVING FUN 26

DANGERS OF FRONTIER LIFE 28

THE END OF THE FRONTIER 30

GLOSSARY 31

INDEX 32

A Frontier School Day

She was up and out of the house before dawn. As the only teacher in a small frontier settlement, there were many things to do before the pupils arrived. A frontier schoolhouse was usually a one-room, log building that had a cast-iron stove in the center. Before the students got to school, a frontier teacher needed to check on the firewood supplies for the day, to make sure that the room would be warm.

Children went to school early on the frontier. Most would wake up at 4:00 A.M. to do a few chores at home—they would chop wood, milk cows, carry water, and help make breakfast. Many students lived four or five miles away from school. To get there they walked, rode horseback, or were taken in horse-drawn buggies.

Before school began, the boys usually bowed to their teacher and the girls curtsied. Then, they would take their places on the long wooden benches that lined the classroom. The teacher would say a prayer and the class would sing. Often they sang "John Brown's Body," "Hail Columbia," or "Yankee Doodle."

The number of students in a class depended on how large a frontier settlement was. Some schools had up to twenty students in a class, ranging in age from five to sixteen. There usually weren't enough students to have different grades. A frontier teacher often worked with one or two students at a time while the others studied by themselves.

On some days, everything would go smoothly. But often the boys in a class would cause trouble. A typical prank that pioneer boys liked to pull was to climb the school's roof and cover the chimney with branches so that smoke would fill the schoolhouse. The penalty for such pranks was usually a hard thrashing with a bundle of hickory sticks.

Opposite: A frontier teacher had to stack enough firewood to keep a one-room school warm for the day.

TRAVELING TO THE FRONTIER

Frontier teachers were pioneers. Like other pioneers of the early 1800s, they traveled to the western frontier in order to start a new life. At this time, the western frontier usually referred to the unsettled land to the west of the Mississippi River. Many of these pioneers came from New England and other

eastern states. Others emigrated from European countries. Once they reached the frontier, most of them cleared the land and became farmers.

Traveling to the frontier was very difficult. Many pioneers walked, while others traveled by covered wagon, oxcart, or buggy. They crossed mountains by following trails that had been made by earlier explorers and fur traders. They also made rafts to travel down rivers, since it was easier than traveling over land.

The pioneers had to choose which of their belongings they would take with them on their long journey. No pioneer could be without a rifle and an axe. A rifle was needed to shoot wild animals for food and an axe could be used to cut logs to make a raft, build a shelter, or clear land to farm.

The pioneers were only able to travel a short distance each day. The entire trip to the frontier usually took several weeks and was very dangerous. High mountains and rapidly flowing rivers had to be crossed. Storms could suddenly make the trip even more dangerous. There was also the constant threat of disease. The promise of a new beginning, rich land, and a better life made the journey worthwhile.

Families used many different types of transportation to reach the frontier.

WHAT THE LAND WAS LIKE

Some frontier families built their homes near forests and streams where wood and food were plentiful.

The western frontier was a vast land west of the Mississippi River that was divided into three regions—the Great Plains, the Southwestern Desert, and the Pacific Coast.

For the pioneers who settled between the Mississippi River and the Rocky Mountains, the land was flat and, in some parts, had wide, grassy plains. On these plains, the pioneers had to work hard to clear the land of thick sod in order to plant their crops and build their homes. In the summer, pioneers lived with strong wind and hot sun; in the winter there was wind and snow.

Families who settled in the southwestern region of the frontier encountered hot, dry deserts. Pioneers had difficulty finding enough water for their farm animals.

In the Pacific Coast area of the frontier, the land consisted of rolling hills and long, narrow valleys covered with dense forests. Through these forests, many rivers and streams flowed. Pioneers had to clear large trees and thick brush before they could build their homes. However, the forests supplied the pioneers with the animals and food they needed to survive.

Hunting wild animals provided many different kinds of meat, including deer, rabbit, squirrel, duck, pigeon, wild turkey, grouse, and quail. Over 200 different kinds of fish lived in the rivers and streams. Nuts, berries, and wild plums were special treats. Herbs were used for seasoning food and as medicines to help cure ailments.

Once the land was cleared of trees, the pioneers found that the rich forest soil made ideal farmland. The abundance of trees provided wood for building log cabins. The wood from cherry, walnut, beech, and poplar trees was used for making furniture. The wood also provided a source of fuel for cooking, and for heating homes in cold weather.

Pioneer men often hunted wild turkey for food.

MAKING A HOME

It was important for the pioneers to plan their journeys so they would arrive at the frontier in the spring. Arriving in spring allowed enough time to clear the land and to raise enough crops to supply food for the winter. There would also be time to build a log cabin home before cold weather set in.

Choosing the right plot of land had to be done carefully. Land that was too hilly was hard to plow. It was much easier to build on a level piece of

land. Choosing land near a river or stream ensured a supply of water that did not have to be carried too far. The land that each new family chose was called a homestead.

Clearing the land and planting crops was the first thing that had to be done. Building a log cabin had to wait. In the meantime, however, a family needed some kind of shelter in which to live. Many pioneers built a half-camp. A half-camp was a simple structure made from tree bark and branches. It had three sides and a roof. The fourth side was open and faced a fire. During the day, the fire could be used for cooking. At night, it provided warmth and kept away wild animals.

Once land had been cleared, and crops planted, a pioneer family would build a log cabin. Since no one person could lift the heavy logs by themselves, neighboring settlers gathered to help. The job was called a house-raising. It took most of the summer to finish building a log cabin. However, by the time cold weather arrived, a family had a warm home in which to live.

At first, pioneer homesteads were separated by many miles of unsettled land. Eventually, as more people settled into a region, small communities began to form. Some people opened stores, and a community often worked together to build a church. Once a community was established, it was time to look for a frontier teacher.

Settlers worked together to build a log cabin home for a new frontier family.

FINDING A TEACHER

When the early pioneers first moved to the frontier, there were no schools or teachers. Instead, children were taught at home by their parents. Pioneer parents didn't spend much time teaching formal subjects like spelling and arithmetic. Instead, they felt it was more important to teach their children the skills they needed to survive on the frontier.

Boys learned to use axes, hunting knives, and rifles. They also learned how to plow, to care for livestock, and to repair tools. Girls learned to cook, sew, and use a spinning wheel, a weaving loom, and a quilting frame. Parents also

Boys learned how to plow their families' fields. Chores had to be done before and after the school day.

Textbooks were not available for students to use either—there were no history books, science books, math books, or English books. Frontier teachers usually asked students to bring to school whatever books they had at home. Students often arrived at school carrying a variety of their own books, including dictionaries, history books, biographies, and storybooks. If books were really in short supply, frontier teachers might have used the Bible, almanacs, and even old catalogs to teach lessons.

If teachers were lucky, many of their students would have their own copies of a popular reader that was called *McGuffey's First Reader*. This book was filled with inspiring stories about hard work and honesty. Some students also had copies of *The American Spelling Book,* which was also called the blue-book speller. This book helped students to learn the correct spelling and pronunciation of words. Sometimes, a teacher had his or her own copies of these books and shared them with students.

Since paper and pencils were both scarce and expensive, students sometimes wrote their lessons on wooden boards with a piece of charcoal. However, the most common material to write on was slate, a small type of blackboard that was about the size of a pad of paper. Students wrote on their slates with pieces of chalk. When they were finished with one lesson, the slate could be wiped clean and used again. A slate that was taken care of could be used year after year.

Some frontier children learned to read and spell using copies of McGuffy's First Reader.

THE STUDENTS

A frontier teacher's students usually ranged in age from five to sixteen. They often attended school only when their chores were finished and the weather was good. Sometimes, students had to skip school to help their families with the plowing or planting.

Many frontier children had to do their chores before leaving for school.

Girls were taught how to sew by their mothers.

taught their children the rules of polite behavior, and how to respect and obey adults.

As more settlers moved into an area, a group of children might be taught by a neighboring woman. Somehow, she would find the time away from all of her chores to teach these children reading, writing, and arithmetic. Most teachers had no blackboards and had to use sticks to scratch out lessons on the dirt floor of a log cabin.

As settlements continued to grow, parents wanted their children to have a more formal education. Families often got together to hire a teacher from one of the eastern cities or towns. Then the community would work together to build a one-room log schoolhouse and classes would begin.

There were few frontier teachers who had any formal training. To become a teacher, all they had to do was pass a few tests in basic subjects. Some settlements were glad to accept almost anyone who would take the job. Sometimes, that meant the teacher was not much older than his or her oldest students.

How a Teacher Lived

Frontier teachers frequently did not have homes of their own. Instead, they "boarded around" with the families of their pupils. They would stay with one family for a few weeks and then move to the home of a different family. Usually, a teacher would stay longest with the families that had the most number of children in school. After school, a teacher often tutored the children she was living with and helped them with their lessons.

A frontier home in the forest.

Each family that a frontier teacher stayed with would provide free food and lodging. Lodging usually meant little more than a place to sleep. Pioneer food consisted mainly of corn and meat. Corn was served at almost every meal. It was made into a kind of soup called porridge and used to make different kinds of corn bread. Most of the meat the pioneers ate came from hunting. Meals often consisted of duck, turkey, bear, deer, opossum, rabbit, or squirrel meat.

"Boarding around" was difficult for frontier teachers. Most pioneer families lived in small, crowded cabins that offered little privacy. Since teachers were always moving from one place to another, they never had places to call home. In addition, these teachers were always under the watchful eyes of the families with which they were staying.

A frontier teacher's pay was low, which was one of the reasons that "boarding around" was necessary. Most teachers

Since they received small salaries, teachers often boarded with pioneer families.

were paid by the number of children that they taught. They usually received two dollars a term for each student. Since the average frontier school had twenty students, the average teacher's salary was $40 a term. Most terms lasted about four months.

Since money was scarce on the frontier, a teacher was often paid in goods. At the end of the term, a teacher would collect his or her salary in corn, tobacco, whiskey, or dried bear or deer meat. A teacher would hope to exchange these goods for money at a pioneer store.

The One-Room Schoolhouse

Early frontier schools were ordinary one-room log cabins with dirt floors. Sometimes, the dirt floors were covered with wooden planks. Many of the schools did not have windows. Instead, a few spaces were left between the logs to let in the daylight. Since there were no electric lights, students needed the daylight to see their books and do their lessons. The spaces between the logs were covered with oiled paper to keep out the cold.

In some schools, wooden shelves that were fastened to the walls served as desks. Students sat at the shelves on three-legged stools. At other schools, students sat on long wooden benches and used their laps as desks. The benches were made by splitting logs in half lengthwise. The smooth side faced up and legs were attached to the curved side of the log. The teacher would sit at a rough plank desk at the head of the classroom.

A log cabin school was heated by a small cast-iron stove that sat in the middle of the room. On cold days, younger students were often allowed to sit closest to the stove. The temperature of a schoolhouse was not supposed to get too hot. However, if the weather outside was really cold, the stove could be kept hotter for the first half hour of the school day.

Students hung their coats on pegs that were fastened to the walls. Other than that, walls were usually bare unless a teacher put up some colorful pictures. Since there was no running water on the frontier, everyone had to drink from the same bucket. It was usually kept in a corner of the room along with a dipper from which to drink. Fields outside of the schools were used for play during recess and lunch time. Bathrooms consisted of an outhouse, a small building that was usually located at the back of a school.

A frontier teacher taught students in a small, one-room schoolhouse.

SCHOOL SUPPLIES

Pioneer children often wrote their lessons on a small piece of slate.

A frontier teacher did not have any of the teaching aids that we have in our schools today. Many early frontier schools did not have large blackboards. There were no charts, maps, or globes for a teacher to use in his or her classroom. There were also no crayons, markers, or drawing paper. In fact, there were no special supplies or equipment of any kind.

In many areas, children thought nothing of walking several miles to and from school. Carrying their dinner pails, books, and slates, they found their way across muddy roads or mountain trails for the chance to learn how to read and write.

A few of the luckier students were brought to school by a family member in a horse-drawn buggy or wagon. Some students rode horses. Because of the long trip, children who lived many miles from the nearest school might not begin classes until they were thirteen or fourteen years old.

Students also had chores to do once they arrived at school. Some gathered wood for the cast-iron stove that heated the classroom. Other students took turns filling the water bucket from a nearby stream or from the schoolhouse well. After classes, one or more students often helped sweep out and straighten up the classroom.

At recess, most frontier teachers insisted that the boys and girls play separately. Boys liked to play marbles and horseshoes. Girls liked to play jacks or jump rope. All of the students played games called drop-the-handkerchief, crack-the-whip, and hide-and-seek.

During recess, male and female students were often not allowed to play together.

21

TEACHING THE CLASS

A frontier teacher had students of many different ages in his or her classroom. There usually were not enough students for separate grades. Instead, a teacher would work with one or two students at a time, while the others studied by themselves. Sometimes, a teacher might ask older students to help younger ones.

A frontier teacher spent a lot of time teaching the three Rs—reading, 'riting, and 'rithmetic. Lessons in American history and geography were also taught. Students read assignments individually, answered questions about what they had read, and drew maps on their slates. Students also used their slates to practice writing and complete arithmetic problems.

Much of the work students did involved memorizing and reading aloud. Students read their spelling and reading lessons aloud to the class. They were often called to the front of the classroom to recite grammar rules, history dates, and arithmetic tables that they had memorized. At the end of the school day, it wasn't uncommon to have a spelling contest like the spelling bees we still have today.

In frontier times, anyone who could do simple arithmetic problems was considered very smart. So teachers often spent a lot of time helping students learn their multiplication tables. Students would practice their tables by saying rhymes like "Four times 7 is 28. Come with me and see me skate." This way of learning was fun and helped students remember the right answers.

When students had learned their lessons at one grade level, they started on the next. The age of a student had little to do with the particular grade level in which he or she was placed. Most students stayed in school until they had a primary education, similar to a third or fourth grade education today.

Opposite: Students had to memorize many of their lessons and were often called on to recite them.

WHEN SCHOOL WAS OUT

At the end of a school day, most frontier children went home to do more chores. The teacher would stay behind to make sure the school was closed up properly and was ready for the next day. Then the teacher would usually return to the home of the family with whom he or she was staying.

After having shared the family's supper, the teacher may have then spent an hour or two tutoring their children before preparing for the next day's lessons. This often involved trying to think up new ways to teach a subject with the few supplies and books that were available.

The school term usually lasted about four or five months. It began in late fall and continued through the winter. The rest of the year, students were needed at home to help with plowing, planting, and harvesting. During these months, a frontier teacher had time to do other things.

Pioneer students only attended school in the winter and the fall.

To make extra money, some teachers spent the spring and summer months tutoring students or conducting special classes. A male teacher might try to make some additional money by working on local farms, helping to build a log cabin, or taking on odd jobs.

Some women teachers spent their spare time learning the survival skills that were necessary on the frontier. Since most female teachers came from eastern cities and towns, many had not learned how to

get along on the frontier. Two of the things these women needed to learn was how to shoot a rifle and how to ride a horse. A rifle could protect them from wild animals and riding a horse provided transportation, which made them more independent.

Unfortunately for many settlements, teachers often moved on at the end of a school term. Those who could not adjust to frontier life moved back East. Others taught at larger settlements where there were more students and a chance to earn a better salary.

HAVING FUN

Frontier teachers celebrated Christmas with the families they stayed with during the school term.

Frontier life was hard and often lonely. Because homesteads were far apart, people had to travel to see each other.

A Saturday trip to town was a special event for everyone, including a frontier teacher. There were often variety shows that had magicians, jugglers, or snake charmers. Also a circus might be passing through or a group of traveling actors might be performing a play at the town hall.

On weekends and holidays, a frontier teacher might have attended a church social, songfest, house party, or community dance. Dancing was a favorite pastime for children and adults. Local musicians provided the music for waltzes, polkas, and square dances.

A frontier teacher usually celebrated Christmas at the home of the family with which he or she lived. Christmas was a very important holiday. It was celebrated at home with everyone taking part in decorating the tree; enjoying Christmas cookies, cakes, and candies; and singing songs.

The Fourth of July was one of the most popular community events, and frontier teachers enjoyed the activities along with everyone else. There was usually a speaker, a parade, horse races, ball games, pie-eating and shooting contests, and dancing.

Children also had the whole outdoors in which to play. They explored forests, raced through fields, swam at the local swimming hole, and often went fishing. Sometimes, they caught wild animals, like turtles or rabbits, and kept them for pets. Whenever cold weather forced them inside, children could amuse themselves with handmade toys or play games like checkers and dominoes.

Even with all the hardships of frontier life, there were many ways for everyone to have fun and enjoy themselves.

People on the frontier often held dances for entertainment.

DANGERS OF FRONTIER LIFE

Frontier teachers had to face the same dangers of frontier life as everyone else. One of those dangers came from outlaws. Many outlaws saw the frontier as "easy pickings." Homesteads were scattered and often easy targets, and there was no one to enforce law and order.

Sometimes, bands of outlaws rode through the settlements, stealing horses and cattle. At other times they would ride through a town, shooting in all directions and causing people to dive for cover. A homestead might be raided for food or anything else the outlaws needed.

There was also great danger from poisonous snakes and from wild animals with rabies. Poisonous snakes often hid in wood piles, under bushes, or in dried leaves. The rabies disease was carried by skunks, squirrels, raccoons, and foxes. Since there was no way to treat rabies or snake bites in frontier days, a large number of settlers died from these wounds.

Fire was one of the most terrifying dangers on the frontier, especially during the very dry months of fall. A forest or grass fire could quickly destroy a homestead, log school, or even an entire settlement. Some

Outlaws took cattle and horses from pioneers who were unable to defend themselves.

A frontier home could be destroyed by fire or lightning during dry weather.

fires were started by carelessness, but most were started by lightning.

The weather, too, could be a serious threat to frontier life. A tornado could destroy a homestead in a matter of minutes. Violent lightning and thunderstorms washed out crops and caused fires. Cold winters were disastrous if enough food and chopped firewood had not been stored.

In spite of all these dangers, most frontier teachers believed that life on the frontier was worthwhile. There was no better place to develop a sense of adventure, courage, determination, and independence. In addition, frontier teachers felt proud about providing a very valuable service—educating the children who would become the pioneers of the next generation.

THE END OF THE FRONTIER

Frontier teachers played an important role in the settlement of our country. Without them, pioneer children would have received little or no formal education. The frontier would have remained a difficult and dangerous place to live without education. In addition, the little one-room schoolhouse provided a place where people from different cultures and backgrounds learned to understand and respect one another.

The pioneers continued to move west and establish settlements until they reached the Pacific Coast. Then, in 1890, the U.S. government reported that no frontiers remained. The world of the frontier, and the frontier teacher, had disappeared.

By the turn of the century, new and larger schools were being built all over the country. In most places, children were required to attend school until they reached a certain age. Whenever possible, students were divided into separate classes. Everyone had his or her own textbooks. Teachers had to have a college education and be approved to teach by state or local governments. The days of the one-room log schoolhouse with its dirt floors and cast-iron stove were over.

With the building of new and larger schools, students could have their own desks and supplies.

Glossary

"boarding around" The act of living with different families over a period of time.

frontier An area of unsettled land that begins on the edge of settled land.

half-camp A three-sided structure made from branches and bark used by pioneers as a temporary shelter.

homestead A home, including its land and buildings.

house-raising A social event during which neighbors work together to build a house.

lodging Providing a person with a place to live for a short period of time.

outhouse A small wooden building used as a bathroom.

pioneer A person who lives in unsettled country and helps to prepare it for settlement by others.

porridge Food made by boiling grain in water or milk until it thickens.

slate A small blackboard about the size of a pad of paper.

tutor To teach privately.

INDEX

American Spelling Book, The, 19

"Boarding around," 14
Building homes, 9, 10–11

Cast-iron stoves, 4, 16, 30
Chores, 4, 20, 21, 24
Clearing land, 7, 9, 10, 11

Frontier
    dangers on, 28–29
    end of, 30
    fun on, 27
    holidays on, 27
    land on, 8–9
    surviving on, 12, 24–25
    traveling to, 6–7
Frontier teacher, 6, 28, 29, 30
    finding a, 11, 12–13
    life of, 14–15
    salary of, 14–15, 25
    school day of, 4
    supplies of, 18–19
    and teaching class, 22
    tutoring, 14, 24

Games, 21
Great Plains, 8

"Hail Columbia," 4
Half-camps, 11
Homesteads, 11, 27, 28

"John Brown's Body," 4

Log cabins, 9, 10, 11

McGuffey's First Reader, 19
Mississippi River, 6, 8

Outlaws, 28

Pacific Coast, 8, 9, 30

Recesses, 16, 21
Rocky Mountains, 8

Schoolhouses, 4, 13, 16
School term, 24
Slates, 19, 21, 22
Southwestern Desert, 8
Students, 4, 13, 14, 16, 20–21, 30

Wild animals, 7, 9, 11, 25, 28

"Yankee Doodle," 4

Acknowledgments and Photo Credits
Cover art by Gene Biggs. Interior artwork by Virginia Kylberg.
Pages 9, 15, 27, 28, 30: North Wind Picture Archives; p. 19: The Bettmann Archive.